# Onstage

A collection of poems and reflections

Alina Ayoub

Copyright © 2025 Alina Ayoub

All rights reserved. This book or any portion thereof may not be reproduced or used in any manner whatsoever without the express written permission of the author.

ISBN: 979-8-218-81113-6
Self-published by Alina Ayoub
Alinaayoub.com

This piece of work is dedicated to all those who have encouraged me to write, think, and create. This is for my mother, Jen and my father, Kal who have celebrated my creative projects and supported me since I was just a little girl. This is for my brother, Allen, who always made me feel like being my true self was the coolest thing I could do. Without my family I would not be who I am today, and I owe them everything and more.

This is for my friends who have read and supported me writing poems no matter how novice or imperfect they were. The friends who support me being vulnerable and celebrate me doing something I love.

This is for my teachers and school librarians who let me be weird, read my strange stories, talked about books and literature with me, and let me eat lunch in the library with them. The adults who validated my importance here on earth when no peer my age would.

Lastly, this is for any woman in this world who has experienced the scariest thing life has to offer, which is growing older and growing up. I hope this makes you feel less alone.

Love,
Alina

# Table of Contents

The Paradox- 1
The Chameleon- 3
The Haunting- 7
The Drum- 8
The Growing- 10
Backpack- 11
Umbrella- 12
Exhibit- 14
Parasite- 16
Collection- 18
My Roommate- 19
After Dark- 21
Between- 22
My Soulmate- 25
Robotic- 27
Surrender- 28
The Sun- 29
Therapy- 31
The Map- 32
Mirror- 33
The Jury- 34
Like Her- 36
Molting- 38
Why Should I?- 40
I Am Her- 43
Only One- 44
What Do You Do for a Living- 46

Forgotten- 50
Mom- 52
Mercy- 53
Onward it Goes- 54
Learning Fire- 56
Bruised- 57
Magic- 58
I Have Lived- 59
Common Ground- 62
Legacy- 65
Fly- 67
Stranger- 69
Patience- 71
The Room You Grew Out Of- 72
All the Things You No Longer Apologize For- 74
My Stage- 76
Intermission- 78
Now That I'm Here- 80
Tables Turning- 82

# The Paradox

Today, a shadow clung to me like an old, unwanted garment.

The mirror reflected a face that seemed both foreign and familiar, a vessel now filled with the weight of days that stretch like the endless horizon.

I stood there, caught in a paradox, neither girl nor fully woman. I am an in-between, hovering in a twilight where my laughter feels like a distant echo, tied to a history I no longer inhabit.

There's a strange comfort in the curve of my hips, yet it whispers lists of responsibilities that nag me. Time pulls at my limbs, weights of expectation hang heavy, and wisdom seems a gaudy curtain veiling my deep uncertainty.

The world waits, poised, to cast its judgement on the contours of my becoming, while I fumble through this metamorphosis, half-expecting to shed my skin and awaken anew.

The childhood dreams fray at the edges, bleeding into the repetitive tasks of adulthood.

With each passing hour, I'm reminded that growth is not an ascent but rather a spiral, a dizzying descent into an identity unrecognizable yet achingly close.

What am I but a weathered leaf caught in the wind, terrified by the irrevocable loss of the fleeting days of girlhood?

Each breath feels both a blessing and a curse—a testament to survival in this strange space.

# The Chameleon

They say I am *too much,*
too grand in my gestures,
too slick with shine,
as if my smile is lacquered on like paint over rot.
As if my joy was tearing at the seams.
They accuse—*pretender, actress,*
But I know this:
I have never been more true than when I am lit from the front,
an audience of eyes like planets orbiting around me.
They say, *dance like nobody is watching,*
I say, dance like everyone is.

When I was a girl, I was rejected and discarded from the armies I longed to fight for,
so, I learned who I had to be to become loved.
In my bedroom,
I conjured applause from my turquoise wall paint,
my vanity was the stage manager,
my bedroom was the theater.

Even in complete solitude,
I lived as I had spectators.
When I turn the page of my book on the beach,
I imagine the lens framing me,
with salty hair and a mysterious allure.
Always, I am seen,
even if only through my own dreaming eye.

With a proper audience I ignite.
I am the flint to their fire,
the flames to their sun.
Their approval pulses through me,
and their disapproval twists my sour stomach into a knot.

I shift and change my skin like it's my religion,
I'm devoted.
I am the person who holds the key to unlock a shy girl's throat, who knows how to draw out the echo stuck in her mouth.
I am, simultaneously, the person who can lie belly-up,

I'm a frog in biology class, waiting to be sliced open by careless crowds that curiosity got the best of.

Yes, I do morph.
Yes, I do echo.
But this echo is undoubtedly mine.
There is a core,
it's a coiled wire inside me that won't bend.
I am a mirror, yes—
but I'll crack and splinter if something causes dissonance.

*Just be yourself,*
my most loyal observers chirp,
and to them I nod.
They don't know that *this* is me.
This is me like light is only light when refracted.
This is me like water only ripples when disturbed.
They mistake my performance for artifice,
and ignore that I've built a cathedral of mimicry.
In this church we value connection,

and to connect with an audience you must understand them and speak to them in their language.

So, if I am built by my surroundings... who am I?
I am a scrapbook, each piece chosen carefully and glued down with purpose.
I am a quilt with stitches from every group of people in a room I walk into.
I am a mirror reflecting what I see in you, and what I feel you need to see in me.
And I have never been more myself than when I am becoming.

## The Haunting

I am in your past. I am in your future. I am the hero in your dreams and the scariest thing in your nightmares. I am in the song you hear, and in the rain drop landing on your lips. I am a curse and a blessing.

Once you know me, you'll never not. I'll make sure of it.

## The Drum

There is a drum inside my skull,
it beats when nothing moves.
It plays for no one but me,
and echoes like a name I didn't choose.

There are diagrams of the brain,
a haunted house in grayscale.
The doctors name different chemicals,
as if pain and darkness is a science,
and loneliness is an equation that can be solved.

It isn't madness,
it is memory sinking its teeth in.
It's every swallowed scream swirling inside a pressure cooker.

I rise in the morning like smoke from a spent candle.
I am soft and I am here.
I hold my own hand at night and feel it warm.

If I must carry this mind,
like a broken clock,
then let it tick in poetry.

# The Growing

The stretching hurt.
My skin was too tight for my spirit.
My bones were negotiating with the future.
But I grew anyway,
awkward and lopsided,
a girl becoming herself without permission.

# Backpack

My hands are chapped with exhaustion,
you hand me your grievances,
and I make them my own.

I carry you.
Slung across my back,
the weight of 100 rocks,
waiting to be placed in accordance with your needs.

But when I kneel,
my structure collapsing,
screaming for help,
there are no hands reaching for me.
There is only wind,
brushing against me with pity.

# Umbrella

I am the shadow outside the circle, the extra seat no one needs. I pull it close anyhow.

So, my hands have learned how to smooth the air before it becomes smoke. I smile so wide and holy that it pains me.

I become their favorite candy and feel pride when they say I am sweet. The night before I violently sculpted myself into shapes that I knew they'd approve of.

I'm an afterthought. I'm the name not heard as the party is planned, starts, goes on, and dies out.

I have no desire to make space, only to be the person that space is made for. Not the umbrella pushing past the wind in the storm, but the one finding comfort beneath it.

I press my face against the window and trace a shape in the condensation with a hand that I wish someone would hold.

I see the others on the outside. I give shelter and the acknowledgment of their existence. I know what silence tastes like and I cannot let them starve like I did.

# Exhibit

I keep them around like a broken jewelry box.
It hasn't completely died out yet,
but the ballerina jerks,
the music skips,
and a scratchy noise bloodies my ears.
I look at them in the glass,
the sign next to the exhibit labeled
*The Compromise.*

They aren't objectively beautiful,
but I have painted them in jewel-toned oils.
I know their cracks and rust better than my own handwriting.
I press my ear to the locked door of their chest.
It never opens.

My hunger disguises itself as patience.
Sporadically, they'll feed me a spoonful.
I thank them as I chew with my mouth open.
I lie on my back like a good,

docile,
thing.

I clip my own wings
to prevent myself from flying out of the museum I hold them in.
They aren't for me,
I'm too clever to believe they are.
I am too full of knowing.
Too much of myself,
to shrink in their pocket,
and call it my home.

But still, I stay.

Living in ruin is a rhythm I recognize.
Leaving would make the silence louder.
Some days being in a cage with my clipped wings feels safer than flying in the open and lonesome sky.

Parasite

It has no interest in the dying.
It wants the full, red-lipped, spine-straight fool who jests
through it all.
It scans with beady eyes like a surgeon,
grinning at the bounding pulse in my neck.
It latches onto me—
its teeth are praise and claws are making me feel
needed.
What was once a decorated house is now gutted.
It eats away at me—
taking my sleep,
my spark,
myself.
It sucks the blood from my veins in the name of
teamwork.
It sews the bite marks healed once it's done.
How cunning,
how clever,
to take and take and make me thank you afterwards.

To my loneliness,

I fear you more than anything,

but you are heaven compared to this.

I'll choose the dark and I'll choose the cold.

It's better to be alone,

than to be devoured while smiling.

Collection

I do not have it in me to forgive.
I don't float like a saint in white drapes,
palms open,
blessing and praying for the beasts.

I keep their bones.
I polish them.
Each moment they lunged at me or another—
I archive in my memories like a file cabinet.

I sleep with the past like a lover.
It's a reminder of a protest.
I wear my grudges like pearls,
each one a perfect and unforgiving moon.

## My Roommate

She lives here too—
this friend of mine,
she's made of tangled wires and whispers.
She paces when I sleep,
and draws curtains over joy.

We don't talk aloud.
We pass notes beneath my skin.
*Eat something. Go for a walk.*
She's always barking her orders.

Some days she lets me dress myself,
but other days she drapes her weight across my ribs
like an old, wet, hand-me-down coat.

I can't hate her.
We share a heart, after all.

I catch her watching me in the mirror.
I see her.

She smiles.

It's not peace,

but it's something.

## After Dark

In the cave of my mind,
thoughts swirl and pile up like autumn leaves,
whispers of my own voice and doubts dart around,
a symphony of ghosts I thought I'd gotten rid of.

The chaos comes during the unkindest of hours,
I watch the clock ticking cruelly as I try to get some rest,
my brain is screaming and screeching,
as I remain eerily quiet as a mouse.
The stream of consciousness reveals secrets I dare not say aloud,
this makes it quite difficult to ignore,
because while the constant activity is a nuisance,
the thoughts never dare to lie.

Between

The others move like thunder,
they're committing to forever.
They are now mothers in milkmaid dresses,
husbands in suits with sleeves too long for their arms.
They buy their home,
nursery decorations,
and white picket fence like a cake,
they whisk their dreams into reality.

Over here, I am unrisen.
I'm a yolk too yellow in a cracked shell,
still longing for my mother's warmth,
in my childhood bedroom,
with pavement scraped knees.

I write because my hand with a pen is my only part that
does not betray me.
The pen is a scalpel,
and I am open,
my skin is peeled back like a page—

don't you see?
No business.
No ring.
No mortgage.
No child crawling around with the name I gave them.

I watch from my window and see them clink glasses on rooftops.
They wear adulthood like silk,
I wear it like a scratchy ill-fitting sweater,
squirming in avoidance of discomfort.
I'm too old to be an innocent,
but too young to be ossified,
I sit in the womb,
not ready to leave,
and afraid to rot.

I have no receipts of my adulthood.
I have no scars from birth,
no corner office,
all I have is my spiral notebook
and the hum of my ceiling light buzzing

like a thought refusing to hatch.

How is it that everyone else is something?
While I am still turning into something?

## My Soulmate

If I am not loved—
not gazed upon like I am sacred,
not watched like a fire about to run free,
then what am I?
What is a body unwanted?

I played the part of the damsel,
thin-boned and lifeless,
wilting against the window opening of the tower I built myself.
I am a bud waiting to be watered with his eyes.

I waited.
Years peeled off the walls like old paint.
My thoughts turned on themselves,
a duel in the dark.
The ending never came—
no sound of hooves,
no glistening of his armor,
there was only the wind and taste of the bitter truth—

no one is coming.
So, I did.
I stood from my bed,
still weeping for a witness,
I laced up my boots,
and I became the thing I ached for.
All my wanting—
the validation, security, comfort,
a sick girl to be cradled,
was a mirror.

I reached for my own hand in the dark and have
discovered something divine.
It wasn't a lover's gaze,
it was my own.
No one has ever loved me as I do—
not as entirely.
I am the knight. I am the tower. I am the flame atop of
it.
Nobody else ever could be.

# Robotic

There comes a day when your dream of what life would be is no longer visible. Your mundane tasks fog the glass, and you begin to forget what was past it in the first place.

The lifelessness of adulthood. It's ivy growing, and stems from the moment you gave up doing what you love the most. You push aside your interests, hobbies, and making time for art.

It's easier said than done to make time for this. Most, if not all our livelihoods depend on going through the motions. We are expected to become a well-oiled machine and are trained not to stray from our scripts.

But if you manage to escape for just a moment the fog begins to vanish. And if you squint, the shapes of the life you want can be made out through the glass.

I am a flower and without these sporadic escapes, I wilt.

Surrender

Every time I run from a light dusting of snow,
I find myself stuck in a blizzard burning with frostbite.

The bullet's path I gracefully dance away from,
ricochets more violently my way determined to hit its target.

I'm in a whirlpool, drowning, in no control of where I go and with no way out.
I can't break free of this karmic cycle,
it seems to find me despite my desperate attempts at outsmarting it.

As I refuse to learn from an experience,
the universe swears on all it loves to make sure I eventually do.

# The Sun

For years, I loathed the sun—
that swollen tyrant, smirking in the sky,
golden and royally untouched.

While I dragged my bones through the ash of myself,
he lounged in his throne of fire,
indifferent to my ruin.

I despised him,
as I did the idolized girls in their clone-like cliques.
They moved like dancers through a world that never
once made room for the lonely,
who were left to suffer in silence.

I hated them,
like I hated the boys with the Wall Street fathers,
their speech oozing with generational ease.
They were all slippery engine oil,
and I was a cold-bellied thing gritting my teeth against
the exhaust.

But now I will become the sun.
I was always warm—
but now I'll be officially sovereign.

My pity will fold itself into a quiet death.

Above it all, I will shine,
not for praise, not to be adored—
but because I can.
And those who wither in my light
were never mine to grieve.

# Therapy

The walls around me are a stale beige.
The room smells like someone else's grief.
She asks how I am,
as if the answer is a bird I can coax from my throat
without breaking its wings.

I've brought boxes with me,
she assures me we don't have to open them all today.

She writes something down—
a small funeral for my shame.
I watch her plant my pain like a seed,
maybe something will grow.

# The Map

Every scar, scrape, and scab I have makes up a map.
I see places and moments where I have lived,
some I grew out of and others I never left.
It maps out history, geography, triumph, and myth.
I'm written in wounds, and I walk like scripture.

## Mirror

It used to spit back at a stranger's grin.
It was unrecognizable.
Now I see my legs standing steady like the roots of a tree.
I see my scars from falling,
remembering the moment I tried to stand up after.
The mirror tells it better now.
It shares the story of a girl who stayed,
bent and broken,
but here.

# The Jury

I see myself too clearly—
I am the scientist and the specimen.
My voice is that of a puppet's.
I think I've mouthed the right words,
but the jury in me is already deliberating.
Too much or not enough.

How cruel is it to live alongside yourself.
To be both the butcher and the lamb.
To flinch at the sight of your reflection,
waiting for it to accuse me.

People love the girl I perform.
She laughs like she means it,
she holds just the right amount of eye contact,
and she nods and pauses in all the right moments.
She's stitched together,
but I,
the watcher,
claw at the seams.

Even silence is loud when I am in it.

God, what I would give to exist without analysis!

But I stay,
watching myself drown from the shore.
I'm always a few steps away from joy.
I'm a ghost of myself in my own body.

# Like Her

I always wanted to be one of those girls.
The ones who bloom without thinking.
They have a golden kind of ignorance,
swan-necked and sure-footed,
draped in silk skin and approval.
The world fits them like a glove.

They are without a second voice in their skull snarling at them.
They are not conscious enough to restrict their movements and overthink the way they bend.
They don't betray themselves by existing.

I watch them and gather them in my mouth.
I swallow their grace as my punishment.
Their lives turn me green with envy.
Beauty is no fun when it isn't yours.

I don't want to become them.
What I want,
is to be free of feeling like I need to.

# Molting

Change doesn't arrive kindly.
I am not ready, and I never was.

They talk about growth like gently unfolding a quilt,
therapeutically kneading bread,
mending the seam without thought.
I know better.

Growth is shouting at myself in the mirror—
*look at what you're turning into—*
when I would rather sleep.

I peel back dead friendships like blistered skin.
I gut myself and dump the contents into the pages of
my diary.

I leave my burning home,
despite its familiarity.
There is no applause when you climb out of your own
grave, only the feeling of accomplishment,

as you see the dirt under your nails,
and hear the echo of the person you were,
begging to be kept.

## Why Should I?

I was an angsty teenager,
but not in the way they say it,
not in the quirky sitcom way.
Mine was a slow gnawing hum of,
*What's the point?*
The question remains today,
it sings in the dark and I follow,
a sailor to the siren,
a moth to the match.

Why should I rise?
Why make the bed only to sleep in it again?
Why should I take care of my body like a temple if
inevitably I'll turn to dust?
Perhaps—there is no point.
Perhaps we are only puppets dangling from a forgotten
master's fist.
But perhaps—
I am a writer,
a madwoman with a pen,

plotting meaning in the margins.
I am a force,
and my words are enough to change another's world.
I walk with intention,
I brush my hair as if untangling the mysteries of this world,
I floss my teeth with a soldier's strength,
I cook as if this is the last meal we'll all be having,
is this not the dance of life?
Adding glory to the mundane?

When I hold the door open for strangers,
it is not a motion to go through without purpose,
it is a ritual.
The swift motion is a silent song to strangers that say
*I see you. You matter.*

I don't know what blueprint I follow, or if it's been drawn blind.
But here I am-
washing my face like today is a new opportunity,
brushing my teeth to take a clean bite out of the world.

I don't know the point,
but I have made points.
Sharp, glistening,
and wholly mine.

I Am Her

Maybe I've lost her,
Until I am reminded,
She is within me.

Only One

The air leaves me, and my breath is knocked out by grief.
Each fresh cruelty is another punch to my gut.
Another monster in human skin.
The world keeps spinning like a bloodstained carousel,
I sit inside it,
limp and helpless.

What use am I if my hands are too soft to kill,
my account too bare to carry the weight of this rot.

Evil walks among us in the daylight.
It shops, smiles, and raises children.

Once upon a time I believed I could stop it,
I thought I was born to turn the tide,
and needlepoint light into the black fabric that covers us.

But I am only one, and the world laughs at martyrs.

If I can't save the entire world,
I'll touch what I can.
A hand offered, a smile at the stranger,
and a moment of mercy when the room has lost all humanity.

If the world must burn, I'll toss flowers into the flames.
I'll name them Love, Hope, and Community.

If I become ash,
let it be the kind that smells faintly of kindness worth remembering.

## What Do You Do for a Living?

I sat for hours checking boxes.
Personality type, love language, skill set,
scoring each column to assemble a paper doll version of myself.
*Tell me what I am,*
I begged it,
*Tell me what I am made for.*

They always ask early, don't they?
The taller people bending low to ask with their coffee-colored breath,
*And what do you want to be when you grow up?*
As if we aren't already something.
As if being something begs for a quiet death with paperwork.
No one says *accountant*.
No one says *consultant*.
We say astronaut, princess, hero,
we say shine.

I was in college at the time,
considering my options.
I begged her for a solution,
*What do you think I should do?*
And she asked me,
too soft and too knowing—
*What breaks your heart the most?*

I saw an image of myself,
eating my peanut butter sandwich in the school's bathroom stall,
unchosen and picked last in the lineup,
a shadow sitting in the classroom,
wondering if anyone would miss me if I was gone.

The image of my neighbor flashed in my head,
his name became a headline,
he never made it to adulthood,
he was swallowed by a mind that would not let go.

The lines across the cashier's wrist peeking through as she reached for my card,

markings of pain, maps of suffering,
and evidence of a moment or maybe years of wanting to be anything but alive.

This—this is my work.
Not commerce, not clamor—
but mending torn hearts with a steady hand.
To find the forgotten and say *I see you. You matter. I'm glad you're here.*

Sure, I like medicine.
Of course, history is interesting.
This does not matter.
What matters is what breaks me.
What fractures the wall of my chest and floods me with ache.
I'll follow it.
I will let it be my guide.

This is my work.
Not the job,
not the check,

not the title on my door,

it is the daily choice to notice a human's pain and choose it to mend.

This is the only calling I find worth answering.

Forgotten

It isn't dying that I fear,
the sterile white sheets tucking me in my bed,
and becoming a hollowed shell.
What frightens me is the silence following death,
the erasure,
your face becoming a blur to those you know.
To be gone,
leaving no trace of you behind.

This fear grows stronger as the hand on the clock lashes
forward and petals fall from the flower of time.
There was once a time that I ripped pages out of my
calendar with the hunger of a girl running towards
something—
a future she was craving.
Now I peel them back,
hesitant to move onto the next.
Now, there just may be more moments I've lived to
count backwards than ahead.

I think that if you are lucky,
some people somewhere hated you a little,
while some in the town over worshipped you like a saint.
A myth, a menace, a martyr.
To be polarizing is to be etched in the minds of those you meet.
A hero in one mouth,
a villain in another,
they both say your name.

I don't fear the soil, the worms, or the pain of my lungs fighting for my last breath.
I fear being forgotten.
I would rather be hated than unknown.
I would rather be witnessed than leave my walls up.
I would rather burn than fade.
Because dying does not come from death,
it comes from nobody speaking your name.

# Mom

She folded her grief into the laundry basket.
I watched her from the doorway,
I was small and moth-like,
I studied her silence,
her strength,
and the art of unbreaking.

Now I speak with her mouth.
Her hands emerge from my wrists when I cook, I
soothe, and I rage.
It's frightening how well I echo her,
how the mirror blurs and names us both the same.

Her beauty in burden,
grace in surviving,
and doing without needing to be seen is magic.
I am becoming what raised me,
and it is not a cage,
but a jeweled crown,
of which I have never been prouder.

## Mercy

I butchered myself.
Each flaw—a plump pig,
laid out for slaughter.
I mistook softness for sin,
my gaze as His,
and wore shame like a second skin.

Today—
I hold my face in both hands,
like it is something holy.
I let myself breathe.
I am not perfect.
I am a house under construction,
but the bones are still good.
The sunlight peaks in.

I forgive the girl who begged to be less,
and I honor her instead.
She walks next to me now,
chin high and perfectly imperfect.

# Onward it Goes

It is quite frightening when you begin to understand.
*You want to grow up so fast, slow down and enjoy your youth.*
*You'll never have the chance to live this way again.*
*Cherish the moment.*
*One day you'll appreciate all I did for you.*
*When you grow up, none of this will matter.*

A child holds the lightness of a feather and once you enter the brutal world, a weight bears on your shoulders like you've been dipped in tar.

You are 10 years old and you are free. You play pretend, bring dolls to life, paint and play with no pressure to finance your life. What once made you feel alive fades into the noise of responsibilities, and everything becomes painfully dull.

You are 14 years old and you are loved. Your mother, father, and perhaps grandparents are alive and well.

They drop it all to come rescue you from school should you have a cough. You open your carefully prepared lunch and find a handwritten note wishing you the best day.

You are 18. When your best friend betrays you, that boy breaks your heart, or you get a rough grade on your paper it feels like the world is ending. It feels like everything is crashing down on you. With time, the knife in your back comes out and you heal. You are left with no pain, just strength. It didn't matter.

As my knees grow weaker, my smile lines cut deeper, and my existence ticks away,
I wish I had listened.
I can only hope my future generations do,
but they won't.
Until their knees grow weaker, their smile lines cut deeper, and their existence ticks away.
The same cycle repeats and they'll mutter to themselves,
*I wish I had listened.*

Learning Fire

I would swallow matches as a girl,
thinking the heat was a curse.
I was told to hide my flame,
but it blistered my throat.

Now I'll speak in sparks.
I burn silence clean.
The world cannot hold me
without glowing.

Bruised

My skin had soft parts,
and my bruises bloomed like violets
under my skin.

But even rotting fruit feeds the soil.
I'm ripe with stories,
that will not die quietly.

# Magic

I carry my faults in a velvet pouch at my belt,
I take them out one by one—
a stutter, a scar, a sorrow—
and I turn them into spells.
What once wounded me
I hold closely as my power.

I Have Lived

As I reluctantly gaze into the book of my past,
I read passages of love, heartbreak, and war,
I flip through the pages fast.

I read about my greatest moments of joy,
hottest moments of anger,
and the millions of tears that have shed,
each chapter is a lesson and carefully turning the pages,
I tread.

Now a few times I have reread the book,
I feel moments of gratitude, slight regret, and give
myself grace.
I've embraced my journey, through every step and every
trace.

For in my book, I have come to see,
that every loss, every accomplishment,
every word and every moment,
has carefully shaped me.

I see the weight in my midsection that all my life,
I just couldn't seem to get rid of.
Then I see myself every year on my birthday,
sitting at the head of my dining table,
after my mother baked me my favorite flavor of cake,
smiling and savoring every bite.

I see that my hands are beginning to resemble crinkled paper,
they reveal my age to all who take a glance,
then I see myself basking in sunlight with my
grandmother on the beach overseas.

I see the wrinkles on my forehead.
Then I see myself raising my eyebrows in awe,
gossiping with my best of friends,
and furrowing my brows,
completing my final exam question that allowed me to
earn my degree.

I see the deep smile lines carved into my skin.

Then I see myself laughing from the belly, every day,
with people who—at that time—mattered the most.

I see my posture caved and feel my back aches growing every day.
Then I see years of myself floating on stage in my ballet shoes,
recalling the steps I practiced a hundred times,
and seeing my mother and father waving at me in the audience.

And it reminds me that no matter how old I grow,
it is such a privilege,
such a delight,
and such a beautiful thing to have lived.

# Common Ground

As a girl,
I found the elderly unsettling,
they were a horror to see.
I would recoil from their paper skin,
their palms were pads I couldn't read.
What could a girl made of static and sugar have in common with a collapsing hourglass?
The universe—with its teeth—picked me up and dropped me into the echoing halls of an assisted living home.
Death loitered,
and often knocked.

I met the woman who likes me to paint her nails a pearly pink every two weeks,
her ritual and her armor.
When I cover her brittle nails with the reflecting pearl is when she tells me the mirror lies.
*That old woman? That isn't me.*

She giggles like a schoolgirl, and I see a glimpse of her as a teenager through her cataracts.

I meet the man who has stories of war in his lungs and memories of love in his album.
His voice grows younger when he names her—
his sweetheart he left at the train platform.
He is still waving at her.

I found the jester,
he was a magician and pulled laughter from air he barely had.
His body was stone, but his soul was wind.

I found the couples—
gray-haired and teasing each other.
They mirror what we think only youth owns.

I see they aren't other.
They aren't after.
They are only me—
further down the road,

with more stories in their pockets.
I am no longer afraid,
I see them shimmering and impacting people like me,
even in the days leading up to their final act.

I see me,
in their laugh lines,
their routines,
their stubborn hearts.
I hope with everything in me that I, one day,
will live and become one of the elderly.
They are more alive than ever.

Legacy

The dead are never gone.
They settle in the marrow—
silent tenants in the halls of my bones.

My grandfather breathes through my father's grin,
through that smile flows kindness,
and coins fall from both hands.

My grandmother sharpens my mother's tongue,
wielding wit like sharp scissors,
snipping people into shape.

At dinner, my brother and I resurrect them.
Our mouths are full of food and myths,
retelling stories like it's gospel.
They boom in us.
Their spirit stretches through our laughter.
Their hearts beat in our chests.

Even now—

I feel them.

They are not gone but grown.

Love like this does not vanish—

it multiplies.

They are not buried,

they are alive within us.

# Fly

Routine is seductive,
but don't you feel your soul scratching at the window?

Your to-do list is a sedative,
keeping you busy but barely awake enough to notice
what lives outside your house.

Leave the dishes in the sink,
your plants thirsty,
your tasks and emails unanswered.

Your bones ache for movement,
your lungs beg you for the taste of air in another country,
your ears grow tired of the same-colored voices your home base has to offer.

Let the journey peel the habits from your skin.
Get lost.
Miss the train.

Try to learn a new language.
Be comfortable with being humbled.

The world wants you to see it,
it's spices like secrets,
oceans like songs,
languages like tattoos,
customs like wizardry.

Do not become the book no one opens.
Go, so the version of you can live,
and live again.

## Stranger

I have spoken great words to the wrong audience,
and still—
I do not regret it.

I'll take your pain and feel it.
I'll become heavier and somehow lighter in the same instance.

There is beauty in a stranger handing you a wound,
expecting nothing but a witness to their story.

I'll never regret the raw unedited truths of a passing stranger's mouth. What we've shared at the bus stop stays longer in me than a decade of classroom lessons.

You can carry their grief.
Not to keep a burden,
but to extend something we all wish for.
To be heard,
To be un-erased,

To connect,
and to be seen.

Patience

I plucked the plum from a crooked tree,
it was bitter at first,
but the perfect color lied under its skin.
No one warned me sweetness ripens late,
and waiting is a form of winning.

# The Room You Grew Out Of

There was a time you measured yourself by that room.
The walls knew all and told no one.
The old carpet, chipped dresser, and door always ajar—
was a witness to all your rehearsals.
It saw your tears that steamed on your hot face,
your sheepish smile in the middle of a memory,
and the skin you shed.

You kept secrets folded in your underwear drawer.
Your dreams were hard to name,
naming meant they were real,
it meant you wanted more,
and it meant a possibility of failure.

But you don't live there anymore.
You visit sometimes,
when things get too loud,
or when you shy away from taking up space.
You sit on the edge of the bed and think of all you ever wanted.

And now, you are old enough to ask for it aloud.

# All the Things You No Longer Apologize For

You are paralyzed in the face of making decisions,
you want it to be deliberate,
whether it's an entrée on a menu or a life-altering
change of path,
you're deliberate.

The way you cry during commercials,
the way you fawn when someone raises their voice,
the readiness to leave if something is not meant for you.

When you need space.
When you need closeness.
When you need silence.
And all of the above all over again.

The way you carry your past like a piece of broken
jewelry,
tangled for everyone to see.

You no longer need to be digestible.

You are not too much or too little.
You are neither.
You are you.

## My Stage

As the lights dim, I hear the hushes among the audience.
Morning spills its spotlight across the floor.
I rise in my gold costume my mother stitched for me.

I turn silence into song,
I am the opener,
the main event,
and the final act.

The audience loves a girl who bleeds with grace.
I do it for them.
Scarlet silk scarves soar from my wrists,
redder than roses,
and longer than breath.

When the curtain closes,
I do not vanish,
I bow to the moon,
throw my arms to the side,

and become one with the scene that awaits me.

Intermission

Now more than ever,
I pause to take in the dew-drenched air.
I enjoy the fleeting scent of a new morning,
the beauty in a beginning.

The world spins on,
people on the street dance in a frantic waltz,
but right here time pours like honey,
thick and sweet,
I savor the earth's pulse.

The background is gray,
but the hydrangea bush I've zoomed in on captures me
in a trance,
I notice and I linger,
tracing the edges of each flower with my eyes.

In this moment I am happy to simply be,
I am whole,
I am alive,

and I am enveloped in a moment in time decorated with petals and a sunrise.
There is no place I'd rather be.

## Now That I'm Here

I thought arriving here would feel like a triumph.
Like finally arriving in a room full of people where everyone understands you.
Where everything finally makes sense in retrospect.
It doesn't.

What I have after arriving here is less glamorous,
but far more valuable.

I know what I bring to the table.
I know how to leave a room without guilt.
I know how to say no and fall soundly asleep shortly after.
I know that people leave—not because you failed—
but because you stopped shrinking yourself to fit in the box holding their idealized version of you behind plastic wrap.
I know closure is a myth.
I know doubt is not a sign to stop.
I know I belong in every room I walk in.

I know I hold contradictions.
I know exactly who I am.

Decades are gone but I am not at a peak,
I'm at a wide clearing,
and the air I breathe in is finally mine.

## Tables Turning

I saw the older woman look at me and narrow her eyes.
I was thin back then,
with full, long hair,
wearing a tiny dress.
I was meeting my girlfriends at the local bagel shop,
and foolishly,
I decided she was judging me.

Years later I am older,
sitting at the same bagel shop,
I have lines on my face mapping the story of my life.
I look up and see a young girl bouncing in,
with full, long hair,
wearing a tiny dress.
She's meeting her girlfriends for a cup of coffee.
I squint my eyes,
not to judge,
but to travel back in time and remember what it was
like to be her
I squint my eyes,

not to judge,
but to hope she cherishes these moments of freedom and beauty.
I squint my eyes,
not to judge,
but to reminisce what it was like to be able to keep in touch with so many friends and laugh without worry.
Oh,
how I hope she knows I'm rooting for her!

www.ingramcontent.com/pod-product-compliance
Lightning Source LLC
Chambersburg PA
CBHW050323010526
44119CB00003B/81